Time Management

Sustaining And Enhancing Time Management: Persistent
Refinement Of Time Strategies, Facilitating
Attainment Of A Productive Equilibrium

Harvey Blackwell

TABLE OF CONTENT

Introduction 1

Wasted Time 6

We All Possess The Tendency To Procrastinate. 14

The Benefits Of Implementing A Regular Schedule In Enhancing Time Management Abilities 23

Avoiding Procrastination: Discover How You Can Start Taking Action And Getting Things Done 37

The Formation Of Habits 53

The Importance Of Optimal Time Management 75

Clarify Your Goals And Motivation 96

Essential Concepts To Comprehend About Demonstrated Time Management Abilities .. 109

Understanding What Matters 146

Time Management Brings Selfconfidence 166

Introduction

Have you ever pondered upon the unique ability of others to possess keen concentration and accomplish tasks surpassing your own achievements? Individuals who demonstrate remarkable competence and productivity, thereby distinguishing themselves from the rest. Do you not desire to pursue accelerated progression as well? I can understand why you might make that choice. We all encounter difficulties in keeping pace with the competitive nature of modern life, where our ability to effectively manage time and maintain focus often impedes our pursuit of achievement. If you find yourself in this situation, there is no need for concern. Through the utilization of this literary work, you will swiftly acquire the skills necessary to enhance your focus and attain an unparalleled level of efficiency. Before long, you shall also become the individual who distinguishes themselves, but in a positive manner.

As the content of 'How to achieve heightened productivity and concentration through laser-like focus' leads you towards self-exploration, you will swiftly comprehend areas in which you have been lacking and acquire the knowledge to effectuate transformation. You will unveil novel strategies to enhance your focus level. Your capacity to efficiently identify and effectively overcome challenges will also experience a significant enhancement. As you develop your skills, you will acquire the ability to direct your attention to intricate aspects that you had previously disregarded due to time constraints or the difficulty they presented. You will acquire knowledge on methods to mitigate disruptions that significantly diminish your efficiency, siphoning off as many as 6 hours each day from your working schedule. Additionally, you will gain insights on how to circumvent the issue of procrastination, a prominent factor responsible for the deterioration of business outcomes, income levels, and worker wages in contemporary times.

In the subsequent chapters, we present to you efficacious productivity strategies, tailored to accommodate your individual lifestyle, which have been indisputably instrumental to the accomplishments of distinguished executives, business proprietors, and prominent figures across the globe. Arranged in manageable subsections, these solutions have been optimized to enhance both your reading experience and your capacity to conveniently locate and refer back to specific sections of interest. As you commence reading, it will swiftly become evident that this organizational methodology is not fortuitous in nature. Instead, it serves as a straightforward technique designed to assist you in honing your attention and addressing the specific areas of improvement in your personal endeavors as you embark on a parallel journey of restructuring and systematizing your approach to productivity.

Wasted Time

Each day, we are allotted a total of 24 hours to efficiently complete tasks and achieve our objectives. Certain individuals possess the ability to successfully accomplish each task they undertake, while others experience a sense of being overwhelmed by the quantity of tasks demanding completion. It is not that we exceed our capabilities, but rather that we lack an established framework that enables efficient utilization of our time.

The concept of "Time Management" has spawned numerous strategies for accomplishing tasks, but ultimately, it boils down to the practical application of eight fundamental principles in our daily routines. These eight principles are straightforward to adhere to and their immediate applicability will be readily apparent.

Numerous individuals engage in mundane activities throughout the day that fail to bring them any closer to their desired objectives or set them on course towards realizing their envisioned life. That is the predicament at hand, the majority of individuals merely aspire to lead a particular lifestyle. Many individuals fail to exert the necessary endeavor to realize their aspirations, despite having a plethora of admirable plans, desires, and ambitions. In order to achieve anything in life, it is essential to possess a clear understanding of our objectives. It is imperative to understand the underlying purpose and methods of achieving the specified task. These eight principles enable effective daily planning and successful execution of the planned tasks. Lack of a strategic approach results in the squandering of valuable time.

~ SEGMENTING / GROUPING ~

I am certain you might be curious about the nature of this practice, and I must clarify that it aligns seamlessly with the process of strategic planning. Blocking or chunking can be considered a method of organizing and strategizing. This approach entails allocating designated time blocks to accomplish specific tasks in order to work towards a singular objective.

A mentor of considerable influence once expounded upon this methodology to me with great intricacy. He applies this approach on a daily basis and has achieved remarkable success in every facet of his life. He elucidated this principle to facilitate an increase in my productivity and the more judicious utilization of my time.

Initially implementing this principle involves commencing with more considerable time intervals to make progress towards a more comprehensive subject matter.

Example

7am-9am = morning routine

From 9am to 11am, I will be dedicating my time to working on the ongoing book project.

11am-12:30pm = exercise

From 12:30pm to 3pm, I will be engaging in activities aimed at developing and enhancing the visibility and appeal of my creations.

From 3pm to 6pm, the task entails conducting sales calls on behalf of a direct marketing corporation.

6pm-8pm = family time/dinner

8pm-9pm = daily reflection

From 9pm to 10pm, I will engage in the process of conducting research for my upcoming literary work.

10pm-7am = relax/sleep

As one progressively adopts this approach, there is a possibility of subdividing these time blocks into more specific and concise tasks within shorter durations.

Example

9am-9:30am = write book

From 9:30am to 10am, allocate time for the task of copy editing a section of the drafted book.

The time interval from 10am to 10:30am represents the written section of the book in its current state.

From 10:30am to 11am, I will be engaged in the task of designing the cover of the book.

Applications can be found on both Apple and Android devices which facilitate the allocation of time in this manner, providing timers and alarms to aid in transitioning between tasks. I have made attempts to utilize some alternatives; however, I have discovered that creating personalized alarms on my mobile device is a more convenient option for me. By setting an alarm, you can avoid the inefficiency of repeatedly checking the time in order to determine when to begin a new task.

I trust that you will be able to incorporate this method of time management into your personal life. However, due to my status as a self-employed individual, a significant portion of my daily schedule is not consumed by commuting or adhering to traditional 9-5 employment. In the event that your employment entails working within a specific timeframe, this approach can still be leveraged. Numerous occupations entail various responsibilities that necessitate completion, and employing time management techniques such as blocking assists in maintaining focus and enhancing productivity, even in a subordinate professional setting. It is imperative to bear in mind that individuals who achieve success adhere to a structurcd routine and meticulously organize their daily activities. Utilize this approach and you will observe a greater number of/ enhanced outcomes!

We All Possess The Tendency To Procrastinate.

I am a fervent enthusiast of soccer and hold great admiration for its dynamic nature, as it entails the generation of numerous scoring opportunities by two competing teams, eventually culminating in a remarkably limited number of goals being successfully converted. It underscores the pivotal nature of seizing opportunities and successfully converting them into goals; such decisive actions significantly enhance the probability of victory for the team. I derived pleasure from participating in this sport during my adolescence and throughout my college years, in the company of a tight-knit circle of friends. During my early twenties, I had a profound dedication to the sport and believed that pursuing a career in the soccer industry would be the most fitting choice for me. Consequently, I aimed to secure an entry-level position within this field. I was indifferent towards the tasks I had to undertake, as my primary focus was to have the opportunity to closely engage with the soccer pitch. Following my dismissal from my initial sales position, I diligently engaged in job search efforts each morning, accompanied by a cup of coffee at my kitchen table. Generally, the employment listings were predominantly occupied by sales positions; however, one morning I chanced upon an extraordinary employment prospect. An opportunity to gain experience in the role of a trainee coach at a prestigious soccer academy.

The best part? They extended admission offers to individuals of my status as a newcomer.

It appeared to be an extraordinary occasion that I was compelled to seize, as I was certain such an opportunity would not present itself again. I was filled with excitement and began energetically leaping on the kitchen floor. I initiated the process of submitting my application for the job position, at which point I encountered a portion within the application form necessitating the submission of a 5-minute video elucidating my background and qualifications. It indicated that it presented my optimal opportunity to effectively convey the reasons why I am a suitable candidate for this position. Subsequently, I would be afforded the chance to participate in a conclusive interview. It was a moment of anxiety as I was aware that this video had the potential to be a determining factor in shaping my future prospects within the soccer industry. I completed the remaining sections of my application, leaving only the succinct introductory video awaiting completion. I recognized the utmost significance of acing this particular aspect, as initial judgments hold a paramount level of significance. I dedicated several hours to devising a strategic approach for acquiring proficiency in the art of delivering the perfect pitch within a limited timeframe of only 5 minutes. I contemplated incorporating a narrative-oriented theme, or captivating the attention of the recruiter through the use of carefully crafted anecdotes or memorable statements.

The Decline of a Conscientious Individual

I experienced an unprecedented sense of apprehension coursing through my being, as I was confronted with the realization that I possessed something of great value that was at risk. I experienced a profound sense of urgency and recognized this as a singular opportunity that demanded my immediate action, regardless of the circumstances. Consequently, it exacerbated the situation. I procrastinated on creating the brief 5-minute video due to my fixation on achieving the utmost precision in delivering the pitch. I was determined to ensure that my pitch met the highest standards, striving for excellence rather than settling for mediocrity. To be candid, my objective was for it to be exceptional and surpass all of my competitors. It was imperative that it be the finest among the selection. Due to my inclination towards perfectionism, I found myself shrouded in a state of anxiety, which resulted in my continued delay in producing the video until the evening meal. I continued to refine a brief script, diligently revising it at frequent intervals, while also dedicating time to practicing the lines before a mirror situated in my bedroom. I found my rehearsal to be somewhat unsatisfactory, prompting me to engage in further practice sessions aimed at refining my performance as well as undertaking revisions to the script.

Surprisingly, one of my acquaintances reached out to me that evening seeking my assistance with his project. Due to his reliance on my expertise, I made arrangements to visit his location whilst refraining from making any alterations to my job application that was open on the screen. I arrived at my residence approximately at 2 o'clock in the morning and experienced a state of extreme fatigue. The following day, I ultimately produced a brief video lasting for five minutes, and subsequently submitted it alongside my job application by evening. After selecting the submit button, little did I anticipate the arrival of a distressing outcome mere moments later, yet it transpired with incredible swiftness. The blank screen conveyed the information that they had ceased accepting applications. I was astonished by the sight before me, unable to fathom its reality, yet there it stood. Due to my tendency towards perfectionism, I regrettably lost the sole chance I had to pursue a career in the soccer industry.

It was within my capacity to submit my 5-minute pitch on the same morning as I completed the job application; however, I made a deliberate decision not to do so. I ultimately succumbed to procrastination, and ultimately, it yielded no results. I was unable to complete the job application and subsequently missed the opportunity for assessment by the recruiter. If the recruiter had scrutinized it and subsequently declined my application, I acknowledge the fairness of their decision. However, my application has not been dispatched or forwarded. This event left me feeling devastated, prompting self-blame to emerge. I was one of the participants involved in the soccer match, specifically as a striker, who was unable to capitalize on the opportunity and successfully score a goal. That incredible opportunity was presented to me on a platter, ready to be seized. My task was simply to position the ball between the two posts; however, I hesitated, allowing another player to seize the opportunity and successfully score the goal. The missed opportunity on my part resulted in another individual's triumph.

The Benefits Of Implementing A Regular Schedule In Enhancing Time Management Abilities

The initial phase in improving time management is to establish a structured schedule and adhere to it. The significance of routines cannot be overstated, as they allow individuals to establish a structured framework for utilizing their time effectively, thereby improving their ability to manage time efficiently. In order to establish a regular schedule, it is essential to allocate time for thorough planning. The most straightforward approach to accomplish this involves taking a seat with a notepad and compiling a comprehensive inventory of the activities and tasks you regularly undertake, thereby embodying your cumulative experience. Certain activities will be fixed, such as professional engagements or meals, whereas others will be adaptable depending on your daily routines.

It is of utmost importance that you possess awareness regarding those activities that you frequently undertake. Many individuals often wake up without intention or direction, assuming that the day will naturally bring them positive experiences. Nevertheless, the day does not simply bestow upon us any blessings; it imposes upon us the obligation to ensure that we maximize its potential. In order to enhance your time management skills and increase your productivity, it is imperative to establish a systematic schedule. To facilitate the initiation process, I would like to provide you with a range of strategies to effectively organize and allocate your time by implementing a well-structured routine.

Create a Chart

By crafting a detailed map and engaging in close collaboration, one can effectively attain a greater amount of time. By formulating a daily agenda, individuals can substantially increase their productivity in contrast to those who lack a plan. Creating a daily schedule will enhance your mental readiness for upcoming tasks by indicating how much time is dedicated to each specific task, bolstering your preparedness and facilitating effective time management.

To devise a blueprint for the forthcoming day, it is imperative to commence by envisioning and subsequently documenting all the necessary tasks and activities. By following this approach, upon awakening the following day, you will be spared the effort of contemplating the tasks that lie ahead, thus saving valuable time. This can effectively optimize your time and enable you to promptly commence your daily activities.

Avoid Social Media Distractions

The prevalence of social media platforms at our fingertips has significantly amplified the presence of social distractions in contemporary times. Regrettably, amidst a myriad of options, it is all too common for us to squander valuable hours engrossed in online platforms instead of dedicating ourselves to the goals we strive to achieve.

When devising a schedule, it is imperative to incorporate a predetermined time frame into your plans as a means to deter any potential diversion from the intended tasks due to the allure of social media. By eliminating the influence of social platforms and minimizing unexpected activities, one can effectively enhance their time management capabilities on a daily basis. In order to assist you in maintaining your concentration, consider employing social media as a form of gratification for successfully adhering to your goals and completing your daily objectives.

Stay Focused

The final outcome you desire to avoid is investing your time in crafting a routine, only to witness its disregard due to a loss of concentration. It requires a considerable amount of concentration to transform your daily regimen into actuality. Upon awakening in the mornings with a predetermined plan, it is imperative to cultivate a steadfast mindset towards said plan, ensuring no external factors divert your attention.

Many individuals establish daily schedules but fail to maintain their commitment to them, resulting in the inability to remain focused. Consequently, despite having mapped out their plans, they allow various activities to distract them and divert their attention. To enhance your time management abilities and enhance your effectiveness as an entrepreneur, it is imperative that you exhibit focus and determination in adhering to your designated daily schedule.

Reorganize Around Time

By structuring your day according to time, you will inevitably formulate arrangements based on unforeseen occurrences that may arise within your daily schedule. Many individuals encounter challenges with managing their time effectively due to a lack of preparation for distractions and unforeseen circumstances, subsequently causing a sense of being overwhelmed and eventually resorting to procrastination. By rearranging your activities according to a well-structured timeline, you will discover that it is indeed possible to successfully complete all the tasks you had initially planned for the day.

Establishing a robust and steadfast daily regimen can greatly enhance your endeavors in managing time effectively. Establishing a structured regimen prevents the squandering of time by eliminating the need to deliberate upon subsequent actions, thereby enhancing one's anticipation and facilitating a sense of predictability regarding the events and their respective timings within a given day. When one establishes a regular schedule, they can anticipate reaping the ensuing advantages.

Greater Achievements

The advantages of possessing a dependable approach are vast, with the foremost among them being the notion that you are able to accomplish more significant milestones in your life. This arises from the fact that you are currently employing your time optimally, thereby enabling you to accomplish more tasks and enhance your prospects of achieving success.

More Free Time

By establishing a structured schedule, one can appreciate the notion that the 24-hour timeframe within a day can be efficiently employed for engaging in activities unrelated to work. Efficient strategizing will afford opportunities to engage in a broader range of enjoyable and rejuvenating activities, thereby safeguarding against exhaustion. Time management does not revolve around the mere management of time to increase productivity, but rather entails efficiently employing time in order to accomplish more tasks within a shorter duration, consequently providing additional leisure time to engage in beloved activities.

Increases Productivity

The majority of entrepreneurs with proficient time management skills can affirm that their productivity significantly increased across all their endeavors. The process of transformation is consistently awe-inspiring and constitutes merely one of the advantages conferred by the establishment of a regular regimen.

By establishing a structured regimen, you can allocate a greater portion of your time and efforts towards accomplishing the pivotal tasks upfront, and then proceed gradually towards less consequential activities as the day unfolds. As a business owner, the level of your efficiency and output will be greatly amplified by adhering to a consistent schedule.

Avoid Procrastination

Postponement is an inveterate deceiver of precious moments, but it can be circumvented by conscientiously cultivating routines. Your daily habits have the potential to mold you into a person who does not defer present tasks due to already being accustomed to the approach. When you demonstrate the ability to effectively resist the temptation of procrastination, you can attain a profound command over managing time and persistently advance towards your objectives. It becomes significantly more convenient to engage in delaying actions when there is an absence of pressing deadlines and lack of structured objectives. Invest your time today in developing a structured strategy and implementing a consistent schedule, thereby demonstrating a dedicated approach towards honing impeccable abilities in managing time effectively.

Become More Disciplined

Success and discipline are inherently interconnected, as one would be hard-pressed to find an accomplished individual who does not exhibit a strong sense of discipline, and conversely, discipline is a fundamental attribute found in those who have achieved success. Developing consistent habits will enable you to cultivate a greater level of discipline and concentration towards tasks that require attention, rather than solely focusing on personal inclinations.

Many individuals desire to dedicate their leisure time reclining on the shore, basking in the sunlight, and enjoying the invigorating breeze. However, pursuing such a lifestyle ultimately impedes one's ability to achieve meaningful pursuits or make progress in life. In order for you to make strides in the pursuit of your objectives, it is imperative that you acquire a level of discipline that inhibits any form of compromise. Establishing a daily regimen at present will facilitate the development of a disciplined persona, instilling within you a sense of pride in your achievements.

Rigorous adherence to routines can be instrumental in integrating them into your daily life; however, once they become ingrained, they will prove indispensable in cultivating a prosperous business. Demonstrate unwavering commitment to personal growth by utilizing the regimen of routine as you endeavor to enhance your aptitude for time management.

Avoiding Procrastination: Discover How You Can Start Taking Action And Getting Things Done

Gaining the knowledge and skills to effectively steer clear of procrastination can be advantageous, yet its impact can be contingent upon the underlying intentions one holds. By deliberately selecting tasks, jobs, and circumstances that genuinely resonate with you, it is possible to acquire the skills necessary for circumventing procrastination.

However, it is also possible to acquire the ability to prevent procrastination by adopting an alternative approach, which I will not elaborate upon in this context. The key to overcoming procrastination lies in engaging in activities that genuinely resonate with one's passions and interests. Reflect upon an activity or pursuit that ignites your passion and that you would willingly engage in without any remuneration.

For certain individuals, this entails engaging in gardening, partaking in computer games, composing novels, or even indulging in activities such as snowboarding. Are you not exhibiting any procrastination tendencies with regards to those activities? Why is that? Procrastination is indicative of not engaging in activities that truly align with your passions and desires.

We have been conditioned to hold the belief that it is not feasible to sustain oneself through the pursuit of our genuine passion. Frequently, we choose conventional professions that do not truly align with our personal interests. Ultimately, there is a prevailing sense of discontent and inadequacy. Are you genuinely pursuing your passion? Would you engage in the same activities if monetary considerations were not in existence?

The vast majority will respond negatively to that inquiry. And when I mention a substantial majority, I am referring to a percentage exceeding 90%. It is high time for you to assume responsibility and conscientiously commence enhancing your life. I am not implying that you must resign from your current employment and hastily pursue an arbitrary opportunity.

An alternative approach would be to commence part-time employment in an area of personal interest, allowing for a gradual pace. In the event that you possess a fondness for coffee, I would encourage you to engage in writing about it during your leisure hours. This can be accomplished through engaging in activities such as blogging, freelancing, or video blogging. There exist numerous approaches through which one may commence disseminating content.

It is indeed alarming, I understand. However, what alternatives are available to you? Would you prefer to be at the end of your life regretting the opportunity you did not seize? When individuals are queried regarding their forthcoming demise, none of them express regret pertaining to their failure to amass greater wealth. All of them expressed remorse for not fully embracing life.

If you possess limited knowledge on how to commence, simply initiate an online investigation. There is an abundance of videos and instructional tutorials available for virtually any subject or task. Having acknowledged the aforementioned, it is plausible to engage in procrastination despite actively pursuing one's passion. This phenomenon typically occurs in instances of being inundated or experiencing fear, thus, I would like to offer a few suggestions to assist with its management:

1. Streamline your lifestyle and refrain from attempting to handle numerous responsibilities simultaneously.
I frequently engage in this behavior and have consequently observed that when I engage in weight reduction activities, I find it easier to concentrate and resist the tendency to procrastinate.

2. Please provide clarification regarding the tasks that you are required to complete.
Formulate objectives and meticulously document the minutest measures you can undertake. Procrastination can readily ensue if one burdens oneself

excessively, thus it is prudent to record a manageable and straightforward task that can be undertaken immediately.

3. Acknowledge your feelings
While one may experience apprehension in exposing oneself, it is imperative not to permit these emotions to seize control. Grant them permission to be present while maintaining your concentration on your own tasks at hand. This skill can be highly advantageous once you acquire proficiency in its application.

Benefits of Time Management
Effective time management is imperative, as it encompasses various facets such as academic pursuits, professional obligations, familial responsibilities, personal hobbies, social engagements, and numerous other commitments. It is also a valuable skill to acquire, as it serves as a fundamental

support for a prosperous professional trajectory.

Superior time management redirects focus from current activities to outcomes, thereby facilitating more efficient and expeditious execution of operations. Being efficient with one's time provides the opportunity to manage activities according to personal availability and preference.

There exist numerous advantages associated with effective time management, and a selection of them are enumerated as follows:

Reduced Stress – Effectively managing your time can lead to a direct reduction in your overall stress levels. Fewer surprises. Fewer tight deadlines. Reduced haste in transitioning between tasks and locations.

Enhance Efficiency – Undoubtedly, enhancing efficiency stands as a primary objective of effective time management. When one possesses awareness regarding their tasks, they are better equipped to effectively handle their workload. You will experience increased productivity and efficiency, enabling you to accomplish a greater number of tasks within a reduced timeframe.

Reduced Rework – Maintaining an organized approach leads to a decrease in rework and errors. Neglected items, particulars, and directives result in supplementary tasks. What is the frequency with which you are required to repeat a task? Or incur additional travel by forgetting an item?

Reduced Encumbrance and Challenges - How frequently do individuals contribute to their own difficulties? Failing to effectively manage one's time leads to heightened levels of interpersonal tension, be it in the form of overlooked commitments or unmet deadlines. Mitigate the risk of self-inflicted challenges by proactively strategizing and organizing your daily activities.

Enhanced Time Allocation - While we cannot manufacture additional time, you have the ability to optimize its utilization through effective time management. Modifying your daily travel routine or completing your tasks ahead of schedule can generate additional moments of relaxation and leisure amidst your busy life.

Enhanced Time Management – Being clear about one's tasks allows for improved efficiency by minimizing unproductive diversions. Rather than pondering about your next task, you can proactively stay ahead of your workload.

Enhanced Prospects – Exercising effective time management and diligently completing tasks leads to an expanded array of prospects. Those who are prompt in their actions are usually endowed with a wider array of choices.

Additionally, fortune smiles upon those who are adequately prepared.

Enhances Your Public Image – Your time management skills will precede you, contributing to a positive reputation. In both professional and personal spheres, you will be universally recognized for your reliability. There will be no doubts raised regarding your commitment to honor your commitments, fulfill your obligations, or adhere to the stated timeline.

Reduced Exertion - It is important to debunk the misconception that time management requires additional exertion. On the contrary, effective time management facilitates a smoother and more efficient lifestyle. Activities require less exertion, whether it entails organizing for the journey or completing the undertaking.

Maximizing Time in Crucial Areas - Efficient time management involves prioritizing one's time in areas that yield the greatest impact. Effective time management enables individuals to allocate their time towards activities and priorities that hold significant importance to them.

Time Management Skills

Time management is defined as the prudent allocation of one's time in order to achieve success in every facet of life. Time management not only facilitates individuals in maximizing the utilization of time, but also guarantees the effective completion of tasks within the designated time frame.

It is imperative to carry out appropriate actions in a timely manner in order to cultivate a sense of esteem within the workplace. Individuals who fail to appreciate the significance of time are unable to achieve notable accomplishments and are never regarded with credibility.

Allow us to discuss several essential skills required for the successful application of Time Management:

Stay Organized

It is imperative to maintain cleanliness and organization of the workstation.

Maintaining meticulous organization of essential documents facilitates their prompt retrieval, consequently expediting tasks and mitigating wasteful time spent in fruitless searches. Staple important documents together.

Please refrain from maintaining an accumulation of files and a profusion of paper on your desk. Dispose of any items that are no longer necessary.

Ensure that stationary items and personal belongings, such as cell phones, car keys, and wallets, are appropriately stored and organized.

Acquire the practice of employing a planner or agenda. Prearrange your day with careful consideration.

Please refrain from jotting down on unsecured or unattached documents. Ensure that you have a notepad and pen readily available.

Learn to Prioritize

Set your priorities. Do not labor merely for the purpose of laboring.

Create a comprehensive "Task Plan" or a concise "To Do" List promptly upon commencing work. Please make a comprehensive list of the tasks you desire to accomplish within a day, organizing them based on their relative significance and time sensitivity.

Tasks of utmost importance should be promptly addressed. Do not initiate your day with trivial matters that do not demand your immediate focus.

Tick off completed tasks. It provides a feeling of respite and contentment.

It is imperative for an employee to possess a thorough comprehension of the distinction between tasks of high and low priority, as well as the differentiation between work that holds significant importance and work that requires immediate attention.

Refrain from partaking in activities that are not pertinent. You will consume the entirety of your day without yielding any results.

Ensure that you possess a comprehensive understanding of your designated duties and obligations within the work environment.

Ensure Promptness and Adherence to Rules and Regulations

Punctuality facilitates the timely completion of tasks well in advance of their deadlines.

Refrain from excessive absenteeism in the workplace. Such a demeanor displays a clear lack of professionalism.

Please ensure that you are present at your desk a minimum of five minutes prior to your designated start time.

Make diligent efforts to ensure timely completion of tasks. Avoid procrastinating on assignments and refrain from waiting until the eleventh hour.

Assume responsibility for one's tasks/job

Avoid limiting your effort solely to the periods when your supervisor is present. Work for yourself. One must possess an inherent commitment to achieve one's goals.

Take ownership of your responsibilities and cultivate the ability to acknowledge and take accountability for your errors.

Once something has been accepted, it becomes incumbent upon you to fulfill the obligation within the designated timeframe.

Exhibit some diplomatic behavior "

Exercise discretion in accepting everything that comes your way. Initiating the conversation with a courteous declination will ultimately preserve your standing in the long run.

The employees should be assigned duties commensurate with their areas of expertise and educational background. By adopting this approach, they will become more engaged and ultimately complete their work within the designated timeframe.

More Focused

Please endeavor to center your attention and apply your focus to the tasks at hand. Please refrain from engaging in idle loitering and engaging in gossip, as it is a misuse of valuable time.

Please refrain from engaging in lengthy personal phone conversations during work hours. Conclude tasks diligently and promptly depart for the day. You will have a sufficient amount of time at your disposal to socialize with your acquaintances or access online platforms for social interactions. Engaging in leisure activities during working hours is not conducive to maintaining a professional demeanor.

Be reasonable

It is not feasible for any individual to engage in labour for the entirety of a day. Please allocate a portion of your daily agenda to engage in conversation with your adjacent team member.

Please refrain from unnecessarily overexerting yourself.

The Formation Of Habits

It is crucial for you to understand this concept as it will greatly assist you in recognizing that your actions and outcomes in life are heavily influenced by your subconscious mind. The rapidity of neural processing within this region of the brain exceeds that of the conscious faculty. As an illustration, upon awakening in the morning, you may not even conscientiously consider it. It just happens. Once a habit is formed, the subconscious mind perceives and responds to a situation by determining, "This is the appropriate action to take in this circumstance!" and promptly engages in it. Negative habits operate in a similar fashion. If one engages in smoking while conversing on the telephone, it is likely that little contemplation is given to the act. You just do it. If you consistently partake in the consumption of a cup of coffee each morning and only experience a sense of vitality after its ingestion, it can be attributed to your established practice of indulging in that beverage.

Ever since you commenced the act of sequentially advancing one foot ahead in your infancy, you have been instructing your subconscious mind on your perception of normalcy within your existence. You have discovered that by sequentially positioning one foot ahead of the other, you can effectively propel yourself from one location to another. You have repeatedly attempted it numerous times before attaining proficiency, yet the skill has remained embedded in your memory without fail. That is attributable to the fact that consistent practice has further bolstered the capacity. Individuals who have experienced a car accident often retain vivid memories of the incident, which can occasionally result in a temporary loss of self-assurance when it comes to operating a motor vehicle. This is due to the unexpected stimulation experienced by the subconscious mind. Typically, one is able to operate a vehicle without experiencing a collision, but unexpectedly, an accident occurred. It should be noted that this does not guarantee a recurrence of accidents, nonetheless, it is sufficient to induce a sense of apprehension prior to entering a vehicle. This is the information that will be retained by the subconscious mind - your newfound response, but solely through repetition. Indeed, it requires a significant amount of time for the subconscious mind to assimilate and acknowledge an action as ordinary. Hence, it is often recommended by individuals to promptly resume control of the steering wheel following an accident in order to prevent the propensity for fear from taking hold.

Thus, what are the strategies for implementing novel and highly efficacious practices?

When one makes adjustments to their conduct, novel patterns of behavior emerge. Bear in mind, your subconscious mind does not act with ethical considerations when it pertains to emotions. It is indifferent to your emotional reaction towards a situation. It simply observes that your response to A involves the action of B. Hence, when novel patterns of conduct are consistently adopted, they assimilate into the realm of the subconscious and eventually develop into habitual routines. There is no requirement for these factors to be directly connected in order to yield productivity, but they should align with the overarching goal of cultivating productivity. So what stops you? There exist several factors that could potentially impede progress:

- Delaying or putting off tasks
- Lack of order
- The apprehension of not succeeding
- The pursuit of perfection
- Insufficient adoption of healthy lifestyle behaviors

In the forthcoming chapters, I will demonstrate methods to rectify these issues, enabling you to acquire 30 new habits that will significantly enhance your productivity rate and ultimately contribute to your success in life. Please be aware that any action you undertake in your life is subject to documentation if it is deemed noteworthy. Engaging in an activity only once does not carry much significance, thus despite possessing generous intentions, it will not aid in the development of a consistent pattern of behavior. It is imperative that you maintain consistency and see things to completion. Furthermore, I possess reliable knowledge that integrating habits with pre-existing ones enhances the subconscious mind's ability to establish associations between actions. In the subsequent chapters, I will provide a comprehensive explanation of this phenomenon.

An adequate understanding concerning the operations of the mind and habitual patterns entails recognizing that they are recurrent occurrences in one's life, gradually becoming ingrained to the extent that conscious thought becomes unnecessary. The subconscious mind assumes control, prompting one to execute such actions. Consider the instance of operating a motor vehicle. Initially, you may have harbored hesitation and anxiety regarding the matter. You were unaware of the correct placement of the pedals. You were unaware of the requirement to check your mirror prior to merging into traffic on a roadway. You were not able to readily ascertain the precise locations of all the switches. If one lacks experience driving in low-light conditions, they may struggle to locate the light switches due to unfamiliarity, as this skill hasn't been ingrained. Conversely, individuals accustomed to nighttime driving would effortlessly perform this task without conscious thought.

Habits serve as the foundation for your interactions with the world. They govern the perception of individuals and the influence you wield in professional, personal, and all aspects of existence. Once you acquire the skills to leverage them for your advantage, you will be astounded by your own aptitude. Therefore, I kindly request that you approach the exercises in the book with utmost seriousness, as they are designed with the purpose of assisting your progress.

The Daemon of Delay: Procrastination

Although there is a prevalent tendency to attribute procrastination to the internet, it is worth acknowledging that procrastination has been a pervasive behavior for an extensive duration of time. Throughout the course of ancient civilizations, individuals have faced the challenge of grappling with the necessity to exercise caution when embarking on romantic relationships. In approximately the year 800 BCE, Hesiod, a renowned Greek poet, issued a solemn admonition against the tendency to "defer one's tasks to subsequent days." Similarly, Cicero, a distinguished Roman consul, denoted the act of procrastination as "repugnant" in matters of responsibilities. Those instances serve as mere illustrations within the annals of documented history. It is conceivable that the dinosaurs were aware of the meteorite's descent to Earth, yet chose to resume their activity of Rock Crush.

Procrastination can be defined as the act of prioritizing less pressing tasks over more time-sensitive ones or engaging in more enjoyable activities to avoid dealing with less desirable ones, ultimately resulting in postponing impending tasks to a future time. In order to be classified as procrastination, the actions taken must have detrimental effects, cause unnecessary delays, and serve no constructive purpose.

What has become abundantly evident since the time of Cicero is that procrastination engenders greater harm than antipathy. Numerous academic researches have consistently identified a positive correlation between procrastination and heightened levels of stress, paired with a diminished state of overall well-being. The act of delaying tasks can lead to adverse outcomes, such as insufficient funds for retirement or overlooking crucial medical appointments. According to surveys conducted by H&R Block, a significant number of individuals incur excess tax payments due to their procrastination in completing the necessary tax-related procedures.

There has been a growing inclination towards procrastination over the past two decades. Researchers in the field of psychology have come to the realization that procrastination encompasses a multitude of factors beyond mere task postponement. Authentic procrastination can be seen as a deficiency in one's ability to exercise self-control. Professionals characterize procrastination as the deliberate deferment of a significant endeavor that we are intent on completing, despite our awareness of the adverse consequences associated with such delay. A lack of comprehensive temporal understanding may exacerbate this concern, however, the inability to effectively manage emotions is frequently the underlying cause of the issue.

Causes

In the field of clinical psychology, an association appears to exist between a self-sabotaging mindset, diminished self-esteem, and anxiety among individuals who engage in procrastination. Nevertheless, the majority of research conducted on individuals who do not require psychological assistance indicates only a limited correlation between these issues and procrastination. Contrarily, procrastination is inherently linked to a deficiency in self-assurance or a genuine aversion to the task at hand.

Impulsiveness stands out as a robust contributing factor to the propensity for procrastination. These particular characteristics are commonly employed for the evaluation of an individual's conscientiousness traits, while irrational beliefs and anxiety are facets associated with neuroticism. The characteristic of being a perfectionist does not exhibit any direct correlation with procrastination. The prevailing opinion is that the primary cause of our tendency to procrastinate is a failure in exerting self-discipline. You understand that you ought to be attending to a specific task, yet struggle to muster the necessary motivation. Experts assert that this phenomenon stems from a disparity between intention and execution.

According to Joseph Ferrari, a renowned psychology professor at DePaul University, it has been observed that although procrastination is a common phenomenon, not all individuals can be classified as procrastinators. Professor

Ferrari has emerged as a leading figure in contemporary procrastination studies and has uncovered that approximately 20 percent of the population can be classified as chronic procrastinators. He provided an explanation, asserting that procrastination is minimally influenced by time-management. Advising a consistently procrastinating individual to simply carry out the task is akin to suggesting to someone suffering from clinical depression that they should overcome their condition.

There exists a prevalent fallacy when it comes to procrastination, which suggests that it is an inexplicable habit or even potentially advantageous. Individuals who express empathy towards procrastination argue that the timeliness of completing a task is insignificant as long as it is ultimately accomplished. There exists a segment of individuals who hold the belief that they exhibit superior performance when subjected to heightened levels of pressure. According to the renowned Stanford philosopher and author of The Art of Procrastination, John Perry, individuals have the capacity to harness the art of effectively utilizing leisure time by constantly redirecting their focus towards tasks that contribute to overall productivity. Psychologists encounter a significant concern with regard to this perspective. They assert that it amalgamates beneficial behaviors such as contemplation or prioritization with the adverse ramifications of postponement. If there are multiple available approaches to advancing in a task, procrastination represents the utter absence of any form of advancement whatsoever.

Ferrari elucidated that individuals who have twelve tasks at hand may come to the realization that the final three tasks ought to be postponed. But a procrastinator may do a couple of them, rewrite the list, change the order, and then make another copy of their list. This is a typical manifestation of procrastination.

In the year 1997, a scholarly examination featured in the journal Psychological Science became the pioneering effort to assess the adverse ramifications associated with the phenomenon of procrastination. Psychologists Roy Baumeister, William James, and Dianne Tice, who were affiliated with Case Western Reserve University at the time, employed a rating scale to evaluate the tendency of college students to engage in procrastination. They monitored the academic performance, stress levels, and overall well-being of the students over the remaining duration of the semester. At the outset, it appeared that there were advantages to procrastination, as the students who engaged in this behavior exhibited comparatively lower levels of stress when compared to non-procrastinators. This was presumed to be attributed to their tendency to engage in more enjoyable activities during moments of procrastination. At the culmination of the investigation, it became evident that the drawbacks of procrastination outweighed its potential advantages. Individuals who engaged in procrastination demonstrated a propensity for achieving lower academic grades in contrast to their counterparts who completed tasks promptly, alongside experiencing elevated levels of both physical ailments and psychological stress. Individuals who engage in procrastination consistently submit their work after the designated deadline, resulting in diminished quality and negatively impacting both their own welfare and performance.

Subsequently, Ferrari and Tice collaborated on a research endeavor that elucidated the adverse repercussions of procrastination. They convened a group of college volunteers and communicated to them that they would engage in the resolution of mathematical exercises upon the conclusion of their session. Certain participants were informed that the mathematics assessment held substantial significance, as it would serve as an indicator of their cognitive capabilities. Conversely, the remaining participants were apprised that the test held no significant value and lacked relevance. Prior to commencing the tasks, the students were allotted a short period during which they could opt to engage in test preparation or leisurely recreational activities. The chronic procrastinators, in actuality, chose to postpone their study efforts solely upon receiving the notification of the test's significance. Upon being informed that it was solely for amusement, their conduct mirrored that of individuals who do not engage in procrastination. Tice and Ferrari expounded upon their findings in the Journal of Research in Personality in 2000, articulating that procrastination is detrimental to one's self-esteem. Individuals who engage in procrastination are essentially attempting to sabotage their own progress and endeavors.

The Importance Of Optimal Time Management

Numerous individuals experience a sense of being overburdened due to the multitude of demands and constant interruptions they encounter on a daily basis. Consequently, the significance of time management in contemporary society cannot be overstated. This guide aims to provide valuable recommendations on cultivating an effective regimen.

The subjects addressed encompass the advantages of establishing order, exercising efficient task prioritization, and recognizing the significance of attaining a conducive mental disposition.

This provides students with the principles and recommendations to effectively adjust and accommodate to the unique circumstances of each individual.

This will be of considerable interest to professionals and individuals in the workforce who believe that improving time management skills is vital for enhancing day-to-day work control, productivity, and efficiency.

Efficient utilization of time entails effectively managing oneself, necessitating the organization and prioritization of tasks.

We possess perpetual awareness of the temporal allocation granted unto us within a twenty-four-hour span.

We have a total of twenty-four hours at our disposal in order to complete all the tasks that are required of us on that specific day.

Consequently, it becomes imperative for us to exercise prudence when strategizing, as a lack of proper planning will inevitably result in the intention to fail.

Strategic preparation is imperative to avoid squandering valuable time due to diversions.

It is imperative to bear in mind that our attention should be directed towards the ultimate objective, the ultimate aim, which denotes the desired outcome we strive to attain.

It is imperative that our emotions, energies, and actions converge towards our desired outcome. There should be minimal allowance for, or limited tolerance of, time-wasting distractions.

Allocate time for leisure and quality moments with your dear ones, while bearing in mind that the time devoted to your aspirations should be solely committed to their pursuit.

Why is time management of utmost significance?

The concept of "temporal organization" pertains to the effective allocation and scheduling of one's time for various tasks and activities.

The advantages of effective time management are substantial:

- Cultivate a Predisposition towards Sustained Achievement

- Determine the key actions that yield the greatest value to optimize your outcomes

Outcomes and Strategy for Achieving Your Objectives

- Achieve Optimal Results through Effective Task Prioritization

Your Time Allocation Strategy

- Establish a Daily Success Regimen and Optimal Objective

Strategizing for Enhancing Personal Efficiency

- Effective Time Management: A Key Solution to Overcoming Procrastination and Achieving Task Completion

Every Day

- Establishing a Strategy to Transform Your Long-Term Objectives Into Reality

Smaller Tasks on a Monthly, Weekly, and Daily Basis

- Develop an Individualized, Tangible, and Methodical Action Blueprint Grounded in Your Personal and Professional Journey

Goals

- Enhance Efficiency to Accomplish Greater Results within a Limited Timeframe

Utilizing Optimal Time Management Strategies

Not effectively managing your time can lead to a range of unfavorable outcomes:

- Failure to meet deadlines

- Inefficiency

- Substandard quality • Inadequate quality • Inferior quality • Unsatisfactory quality • Deficient quality

- Negative professional standing

- Increased levels of stress • Heightened stress • Elevated levels of stress • Augmented stress levels • Intensified stress

Inadequate time management skills can significantly diminish your productivity, consequently leading to missed opportunities, such as hindered progress in professional advancement.

By effectively optimizing your time management skills, you establish an affirmative pattern and cultivate a routine conducive to achieving success.

You will experience enhanced professional performance, seize greater prospects, enjoy increased leisure time, and attain a heightened state of overall well-being.

The cultivation of exemplary time management abilities considerably enhances various facets of one's life. Merely commence the task at hand!

Chapter 1:

Creating a Schedule

Have you ever pondered the underlying cause behind the disparity in productivity levels observed between certain individuals who effortlessly accomplish a multitude of tasks within a single day, whilst you find yourself grappling to complete your own obligations, thereby experiencing a sense of inadequacy and a persistent lag in progress? Did you ever contemplate that this might be the final instance in which you succumb to the temptation of delaying a project, only to discover that you inevitably engage in procrastination shortly after making such a resolution to yourself?

Similar to the majority of individuals, I personally encountered challenges with the persistent tendency to procrastinate over an extended duration. I am engaged in remote work, where I operate independently without superiors or direct supervision. I would delay the progress of my projects until the final moment, thereby subjecting myself to a myriad of stress and anxiety. I would abstain from formulating strategies for unpredictable circumstances, an approach that frequently gives rise to various complications for me. I would advise myself against procrastinating on tasks and instead urge myself to complete them proactively to avoid being overwhelmed by an excessive workload. I would postpone it to a later date and subsequently experience a sense of remorse. This feeling of guilt only further facilitated my inclination to postpone tasks.

If you find yourself resonating with the aforementioned description, this book is precisely tailored to meet your needs. Engaging with the tips and techniques presented herein will be pivotal, as the insights I will provide have the potential to significantly enhance your experience.

1. Compile a comprehensive inventory of tasks you aim to accomplish within a single day. Do not concern yourself with any temporal limitations during your initial efforts; simply compile a comprehensive list encompassing all your desired tasks.

2. Develop a chronological plan for the activities you will engage in throughout the day. This concept is, in fact, quite straightforward. To effectively commence, please acquire a sheet of notebook paper that contains evenly spaced lines, subsequently formulating a chronological diagram delineating the events unfolding from the moment of

awakening, exemplifying the following structure:

5:00-

6:00-

7:00-

Please leave a blank line between each hour to indicate the half hour mark. Please ensure that all 24 hours are included on this page. After successfully creating this, it is imperative to subsequently refer to your list. What are the key tasks that require your attention and what obligations are unavoidable? For example, your job. It is mandatory for you to attend work on a daily basis. This matter holds significant importance, and unless your financial means are exceedingly abundant, it is necessary for you to address it. Mark out the time that you will be at work, start by drawing a straight line like this – and one on the hour that you get off of work. Create a vertical line to establish a direct connection between the previously drawn lines.

Subsequently, you will proceed to delineate the duration dedicated to rest using an identical methodology. All that remains is what you must utilize.

3. Now, it is imperative to assess your agenda of objectives and juxtapose it with the remaining time at your disposal. You are now required to incorporate activities such as morning hygiene and meal preparation. In order to accomplish any task on a typical

workday, it is necessary to allocate a specific time for its completion.

This will leave you with a limited amount of time remaining, during which you may schedule appointments with healthcare professionals, engage in leisure activities, or attend to any other tasks and responsibilities you have throughout the day. Suppose you dedicate 10 hours daily to work, allocate 8 hours for sleep, require 1 hour to prepare for work and ensure your children depart for school, and set aside 1 hour daily for meal preparation and consumption. At present, you are endowed with a remaining duration of four hours. What is the utmost significant task that requires your attention throughout that four-hour period? What tasks or responsibilities have you been postponing? Are you engaged in the task of tidying your residence or tending to the laundering of garments? Perhaps it involves landscaping maintenance or performing routine maintenance on your vehicle. It is imperative that you prioritize the most essential task and place it at the top of your list.

4. Allocate an additional 25 percent of time to your schedule compared to your initial estimate for the completion of the task. As an illustration, when estimating the time required for housecleaning, it is advisable to allocate one hour and fifteen minutes if you initially anticipated a one-hour duration. This will guarantee that you do not experience time constraints.

This is among the factors that greatly contributed to my progress. In the context of remote work, it is imperative to possess the capability to accurately gauge the time required to complete a given task. I estimate that completing a job would require approximately four hours, disregarding any potential complications. To allow for such contingencies, I would conscientiously allocate sufficient work to accommodate a span of 10 hours, but often find myself dedicating 12 to 14 hours to complete the task. After acquiring the knowledge that additional time allocation was imperative for the tasks at hand, significant improvements in the outcome ensued. If the time allocated for the first task is not necessary, you may expedite the commencement of the second task, thus acquiring an advantageous temporal buffer.

5. Acquire a pristine, brand-new notebook. Designate a previously unused document and unequivocally refer to it as a daily itinerary. In this literary piece, the reader will delineate a comprehensive agenda for each successive day over the course of the ensuing week.

In a similar vein to your previous task of creating the schedule for a typical day, you will now be responsible for documenting and specifying the precise activities that will occur during each interval, noting their respective timings. This notebook is intended to remain in your possession at all times, ensuring that in the event of an appointment, you won't have to rely on your memory and risk mistakenly double-booking or overlooking it. Each week, it is expected that you will devise a comprehensive plan for the upcoming week, taking into account any pre-existing commitments. During the remaining time, you will engage in addressing the tasks that you have been delaying.

6. Consider the financial implications of your procrastination. This experience held significant importance in my life. I tended to engage in postponement during the initial two weeks of the month, subsequently necessitating an intensified effort during the final two weeks to reconcile my financial obligations. I ultimately fell behind and experienced a sense of inadequacy. I grew weary of living in such a manner

and found it imperative to question the repercussions of my procrastination. If you are consistently late when it comes to paying your bills, it could be that you are lowering your credit score, you could be paying a bunch of late fees that could have been avoided and adding more stress into your life. Take into account the potential alteration in your emotions and the consequential reduction in expenditure of time and resources if you were to cease the habit of procrastination.

Primarily, do not perceive yourself as being trapped. Regardless of the duration of your procrastination, it is possible to transform yourself if you possess sincere determination. You simply need to commence with modest strides. In the subsequent chapter, we shall delve into the reasons behind individual tendencies towards procrastination and propose suitable strategies for amending such behavioral patterns.

Clarify Your Goals And Motivation

Effective time management and improvement is contingent upon the presence of personal goals that drive the desired change. Insufficient would it be if your boss, spouse, or friends find themselves vexed by your habits.

What are your anticipated benefits of improved organization - such as increased financial gains, enhanced professional reputation, higher social standing, or an overall improvement in your quality of life?

Any of the aforementioned aspirations, among innumerable others, are capable of compelling an individual to enact substantial alterations to their efficacy and systemization. Nevertheless, that is the stipulation: objectives exclusive to oneself.

SMART goals

Now that you have identified the underlying purpose behind your pursuit of mastering to-do lists and how they positively impact your overall life, you may now embark on the journey towards achieving SMART goals. Indeed, this implies pursuing objectives that are prudent to strive for, yet it also carries considerable significance in assigning meaning to every set goal.

These goals are:

• Precise - The Five W's are relevant in this context. Ensure that you possess the ability to provide comprehensive responses to the inquiries of Who, What, When, Where, and Why in relation to the objective.

• Quantifiable – Establish a pre-determined method to assess the attainment of your objectives, employing a specific benchmark to gauge the extent to which you have achieved your intended outcomes.

• Feasible – Considering your schedule and the various dimensions of your life, do you perceive this as achievable? If that is not the case, it is necessary to revise the draft.

• Applicable - The goals you establish are designed to be advantageous to you. Consequently, refrain from pursuing accolades in a field that fails to pique your interest solely for the purpose of impressing someone. Do things you can be proud of and set goals accordingly.

• Punctuality - Adherence to a designated timeframe for achievement, along with the capacity to confidently affirm the successful attainment of said goal, is imperative in this context.

An alternative formulation to describe the same concept in a formal tone would be: "A supplementary approach to delineating objectives, as presented in the acclaimed literary work, Made to Stick authored by Chip Heath and Dan Heath, is SUCCES—an acronym denoting the concept of sticky goals." These goals are:

• Easy to understand - The fundamental concept can be readily conveyed.

• Unexpected – Out of the ordinary or not "the norm."

• Ideas that are accompanied by a wealth of specific details tend to have a lasting impact. Tales that have been transmitted over the course of generations serve as excellent illustrations.

• Credible – It could be deemed believable if it were to happen to someone else.

• Narratives evoking emotions – You display empathy towards the individuals portrayed in the narrative.

Now, the question arises as to how precisely this set of criteria can be applied to the goals outlined in your to-do list? It can be stated in a formal tone as follows: "To put it plainly, these particular objectives manage to capture one's attention." Evidently, the act of sending emails to the team fails to evoke the same level of attention and enthusiasm as the creation of a new piece of art or the development of an advertising campaign for a cause you hold strong convictions in. Therefore, when formulating your objectives, it is advisable to consider these criteria, while keeping in mind that they need not necessarily be present in every goal. This brings a sense of novelty to your thought process and, at the least, facilitates your personal development to encompass a broader range of perspectives.

It is of utmost importance to divide a significant objective into more manageable and attainable sub-objectives. This task is more conducive to measurement and scheduling, thereby enabling diligent monitoring of one's progress towards achieving the overarching objective. Lacking tangible measures for achieving a significant objective enhances the likelihood of being sidetracked and prone to delaying progress.

Breaking down the tasks leading up to the ultimate deadline into smaller increments facilitates periodic breaks for rejuvenation or to obtain minor incentives along the way towards achieving the larger objective.

What is impeding your progress?

It is imperative to attend to the factors that impede your productivity level. Initially, compile a catalog of the foremost obstacles that typically impede your progress when endeavoring to complete tasks outlined in your agenda. In the event that you are initiating the implementation of to-do lists, consider compiling a record of activities or circumstances that frequently divert your attention for a minimum of two days per week.

Interruptions have the potential to consume up to two hours of your daily time. This entails a substantial reduction in the overall allocated time for the purpose of being efficient.

Based on an average U.S. Lifespan of 79 years, if you were to dedicate two hours per day, seven days per week, and 52 weeks per year to distraction, your total accumulated time spent being distracted would amount to approximately 57,512 hours. Clearly, by exerting some level of diligence, it is possible to allocate at least a portion of that time towards more fruitful endeavors.

Social media is presently a prominent hindrance, diversion, and obstacle to effective time management. The utilization of diverse communication channels enables swift and convenient connectivity amongst team members, ultimately yielding advantageous outcomes. The capability to conduct research on the go is undoubtedly superior to being confined to a library for extended periods, merely to discover that the concept you are exploring lacks substance. Nevertheless, the drawback of these evident advantages lies in the availability of unnecessary commodities.

There is no rationale behind maintaining daily contact with friends or former high school acquaintances on the Facebook platform. There is no inherent necessity to be promptly notified, either through a notification or email, about receiving an invitation to partake in a game across various social media platforms.

Ultimately, it is unnecessary for every individual to have prompt access to their email on a constant basis. Indeed, certain crucial business transactions are successfully carried out through the transmission of documents via electronic mail. Certainly, it holds true that negotiations can also be conducted through electronic mail. Nevertheless, for the majority of individuals, constantly monitoring email at intervals of two minutes or reacting to each gentle notification noise is merely hindering the progress we could make towards accomplishing the task at hand or the development of a nascent idea within a collaborative thinking session.

Natural Tendencies vs. The Conventional Approach" "The Established Method" "The Widely Accepted Practice

Have you observed whether you achieve tasks with greater ease during the morning or the evening? Allocate a specific period to accomplish these tasks during the time when your chances of successfully completing them are highest. Not everyone possesses the inherent suitability for adhering to the conventional 9 to 5 work schedule, or even achieving prosperity exclusively in diurnal circumstances. If you have a propensity for higher levels of creativity or ambition during the afternoon or evening, it is inadvisable to exert undue effort in the morning. The outcome will be unfavorable to your interests.

Furthermore, endeavor to meticulously structure your schedule to ensure the attainment of triumph. If you are aware of your tendency to have a slower start in the morning but exhibit higher levels of productivity after lunch, it would be advisable to formulate your to-do list in a manner that incorporates less demanding tasks during the morning hours, and reserves the majority of your responsibilities for completion in the afternoon.

Discovering one's personal strengths holds immense significance for a multitude of reasons in the course of one's life. Understanding your areas of greatest enthusiasm and exceptional aptitude proves to be equally instrumental in achieving success, alongside possessing attributes of organization and productivity. Employ innovative thinking to identify the optimal strategies for approaching a task or the specific domains within the task where your strengths lie. Subsequently, it is crucial to prioritize emphasizing your strengths in any given scenario while allocating additional time to those aspects that are acknowledged as beyond your domain of expertise.

Essential Concepts To Comprehend About Demonstrated Time Management Abilities

Similarly to currency, time must be managed adeptly. If one effectively allocates and monitors their time, they can achieve the optimal equilibrium between professional obligations, recreational pursuits, and periods of relaxation. You effectively achieve what is most important in your life. Furthermore, this practice can effectively decrease stress levels and substantially enhance overall well-being, leading to heightened levels of happiness. In order to aid you in effectively managing your time, we present to you ten demonstrated skills in time management that are imperative for acquisition at this present moment.

Settings Goals

Why is the establishment of personal goals imperative for effective personal time management? From a perspective of time management, one's life can be characterized as a series of significant and minute decisions and choices. It is the choices that you genuinely manage, rather than the passage of time.

Creating an effective system for personal goal setting necessitates a thorough understanding of technical expertise and an in-depth knowledge of psychology. This knowledge will enable individuals to effectively guide their subconscious and conscious decision-making processes, ultimately increasing motivation and facilitating the achievement of individual or corporate objectives.

Objectives offer individuals a clear, directed, and predetermined target to strive towards. They facilitate the development of a well-defined mindset regarding one's desired goals and provide guidance on effectively managing one's time and resources to achieve them. Through the establishment of objectives, one can discern the value of allocating time and the importance of avoiding distractions.

Commence by inquiring within yourself as to your desired destination within a span of six months. One could potentially extend their perspective and contemplate their desired future state for the subsequent year or even decade henceforth. Establish individual objectives that are both feasible and achievable. This can serve as a crucial step in ensuring effective time management.

Acquire knowledge regarding what you aim to achieve. Please craft a concise definition of your objective within a single sentence. Please endeavor to revise this specific sentence until it becomes unmistakably clear and concise.

Prior to retiring for the night and upon awakening, it is recommended to peruse this sentence multiple times.

Take a few moments, multiple times throughout the day, to imagine your desired outcome. In your perspective, consider your objective as attained.

Preserve a state of anticipation and cultivate a receptive attitude. This can promote attentiveness and mindfulness towards suggestions and opportunities that may arise, facilitating the recognition and achievement of your desired objective.

Harness your personal determination and exhibit exceptional self-control to preserve unwavering concentration towards your objective, as well as steadfastly adhere to your commitment in order to achieve triumph. Do not allow any distractions or inconveniences to undermine your focus and steer you away from your intended objective.

Continue forward despite encountering obstacles or experiencing a lack of progress. Those who demonstrate perseverance ultimately emerge victorious.

Silence will be electricity. Try to refrain from elaborating excessively on your aspirations. Direct your attention towards action rather than mere verbal expression. Excessive discourse with others regarding your needs and objectives significantly diminishes your inherent capabilities. Acquire the skills necessary to concentrate and direct your energy towards achieving your desired goal.

Chapter 07: Embracing Proactivity

Taking preemptive action before a situation escalates into a state of emergency is referred to as being proactive. In order to exhibit proactivity, individuals must possess a cognizance of forthcoming circumstances, enabling them to capitalize on favorable opportunities that lie ahead. Lacking this level of awareness makes it challenging to take proactive measures in any given circumstance. Individuals who demonstrate proactivity tend to exhibit traits of precision, speculation, and organization.

The concept of a proactive approach can be illustrated through a common everyday scenario.

John and Iqbal are two acquaintances residing in closely situated towns separated by a distance of approximately 40 kilometers. One day, they engaged in a telephonic conversation and agreed to embark on a leisurely excursion to a nearby destination the following morning. An agreement was reached for Iqbal and his wife to join together with John at his residence, whereupon the two families would proceed in John's vehicle for the excursion.

The following morning, as John awaited the arrival of the Iqbal family, he placed a telephone call to Iqbal inquiring about the tardiness of their arrival. Iqbal expressed his disappointment as he discovered that his car tire had deflated, and he was unable to replace it as he soon realized that the spare tire was also deflated. He had requested transportation and proceeded to a nearby establishment specializing in tire repairs. In a brief while, he would make his way back to his vehicle, undertake the task of replacing the tire, and subsequently resume his journey. In the interim, his family was compelled to tarry within the vehicle in a state of disrepair.

The entire event resulted in an unforeseen loss of two hours. They opted to postpone their tour given that it would be impractical to return within the designated timeframe. A scheduled recreational journey was transformed into a ruined day for two households. An entire day was forfeit.

John inquired whether one adheres to a proactive approach.

What is the intended meaning behind the term 'proactive'? Iqbal inquired, requesting John, 'What course of action would you have pursued had you been in my position?'

I would have conducted an inspection yesterday to assess the tire pressure and condition of the spare tire. In the event of a punctured tyre, I would have promptly replaced the tyre within a span of 10 minutes before resuming my journey. All of this could have been prevented if, instead of requesting transportation, one had taken the initiative to transport two tires to the nearby tire shop within a span of two hours. Besides, Mrs. Iqbal would have avoided being marooned on the thoroughfare. All of that was merely a brief period of proactive engagement to assess if all the necessary elements were aligned to accommodate a journey. Additionally, I would have taken the necessary measures to ensure the presence of a comprehensive medical aid kit within the vehicle, in addition to ensuring that the levels of engine oil, gasoline, and coolant were adequately maintained.

A proactive approach encompasses any independently taken measures that equip individuals to effectively respond to future demands and challenges. The quality of being proactive is widely acknowledged as an esteemed characteristic within an individual, team, or entity. "In sharp contrast to the reactive paradigm, which defers action until the future unfolds,

It entails proactive engagement rather than passively awaiting events and merely responding to them.

The subsequent instances showcase proactive conduct.

Autonomy Setting and Respecting Targets Preempting Concerns Honing Skills

Insights Gained from Project Management Experience Evaluating Risk and Building Resilience

Strategic Planning Rigorous Quality Assurance Proactive Approach Effective Communication

Tenacity   Determination   Resilience Perseverance Endurance

Technique 6 - Establishing Priority

In order to achieve greater efficiency in daily tasks, it is essential to prioritize and differentiate between matters of significance and those requiring immediate attention. This will enable you to compile a roster of priorities that you can systematically strive to achieve.

One method that can assist you in determining your priorities is to obtain a sheet of paper and proceed to fold it in half, followed by folding it in half once more, creating four distinct compartments. Please designate the columns as Important and Not Important, and subsequently assign the rows as Urgent and Not Urgent. Next, consider the daily tasks at hand and proceed to organize them by categorizing and allocating each one into its respective compartments.

Upon completion, it is imperative that the tasks contained within the Important and Urgent category occupy the highest position on your list of priorities, followed by the Urgent and Not Important tasks. Subsequently, the tasks falling under the Important and Not Urgent category should be addressed, and finally, the tasks categorized as Not Important and Not Urgent. Incorporate recreational activities, such as engaging in television viewership or participating in video game sessions alongside companions, alongside household responsibilities such as completing the laundry. In this manner, you will acquire the knowledge of which options to discard and which to retain.

Based on the outcomes derived from your lists, you can subsequently formulate a comprehensive plan encompassing all the tasks for the entire week.

Skill 7 - Utilize the Pareto Principle

The 80/20 rule is a time-tested and widely implemented approach that enables individuals to optimize their time and enhance their productivity. The origins of this can be traced back to 1906, when Vilfredo Pareto pioneered its development. This implies that the vast majority of the result (80 percent) can be attributed to a select minority of factors (20 percent).

In order to implement this principle of time management, the initial step is to evaluate the predominant allocation of your time. Next, proceed to analyze the correlation between the number of hours invested and the outcomes achieved.

Subsequently, kindly respond to the following inquiries: To what extent did you allocate your active hours towards generating such outcomes? During which period of the day were you most productive? And what can be said about the employees who demonstrate the lowest levels of productivity? What hindered your ability to maintain consistent productivity?

Once you have discerned the period during which your productivity is at its peak, you can capitalize on that specific timeframe to engage in activities that will propel you towards the attainment of your objectives. For example, let us consider the scenario where your objective is to successfully complete an examination. If you are aware of your peak productivity window being between the hours of 10 am and 12 noon, it would be beneficial for you to allocate your study time specifically within this time frame.

Chapter 4: My Attention Was Diverted

Surprisingly, inefficient Time Management or procrastination is not a recent phenomenon. The internet is frequently cited as a scapegoat for individuals' diminished attention spans; however, research indicates that people have been engaging in procrastination long before the advent of the internet.

There are various factors that contribute to your distractions, and currently, the internet is undoubtedly at the forefront, closely followed by television.

Presented below are a few strategies to mitigate the tendency to procrastinate due to distractions:

Eliminate the sources of diversion.

Prioritize eliminating the sources of distractions. Possible revision: "Potential distractions encompass various stimuli such as the television, your canine companion, or your engagement with social media, capable of interrupting your ongoing tasks." Now, the approach you employ to mitigate the disturbance may differ depending on the nature of the distraction. For instance, should the issue lie with the television, one could easily relocate to an environment where watching television is not feasible. The coffee shop or the library are both excellent environments conducive to promoting concentration.

If one is preoccupied by online distractions, the same principle applies. The issue at hand, however, pertains to the scenario of requiring internet access for work-related tasks. Certain individuals choose to restrict access to specific websites on their personal computers in order to avoid succumbing to temptation and indulging in browsing activities. An alternative approach could be to consider the deactivation of your Facebook account or any other social media accounts. If feasible, would it be possible for you to delete it entirely?

Glass Paneling

It would be advantageous to establish a designated area solely for the purpose of work. Naturally, that is indeed the primary purpose behind the provision of an office or cubicle in a professional setting. However, what recourse remains if one continues to face challenges in achieving their tasks?

It is common for contemporary organizations to employ glass partitions for office spaces. The objective at hand is to facilitate clear visibility into the activities undertaken by their employees throughout working hours. If the employees are made aware of constant surveillance, they are more prone to directing their attention towards their responsibilities.

One can employ the identical principle but make slight adjustments if transparent paneling is unavailable. As an illustration, one may opt to position a mirror strategically to enable self-observation while engaged in professional tasks. Certain individuals have observed that the act of witnessing themselves engage in productive activities serves as a catalyst for further motivation to persist in their work.

Productivity Office

There are businesses today catering to people who need a quiet place to do their work. They offer a designated workspace along with internet connectivity, as well as complementary refreshments, creating an environment conducive to concentrated work free from disruptions and extraneous influences. It is a relatively recent concept; however, numerous cities now possess such amenities. Frequently, these offices are leased at an hourly or daily rate. Individuals who utilize such devices typically consist of students, freelancers, or office professionals who encounter difficulties in completing their assigned tasks within their respective work environments.

YOU'RE BEING DISTRACTED

Certain individuals have the ability to counteract the process of distraction by openly addressing the matter at hand. Merely acknowledging and acknowledging to oneself the act of procrastination is a potent catalyst for its complete cessation. It is imperative that you refrain from merely pondering the thought internally; instead, you must articulate it audibly: "I am engaging in procrastination" and subsequently elucidate the underlying reasons for your behavior. By engaging in this practice, you will gain a heightened awareness of the absurdity of your actions and will be more inclined to actively strive for improved time management.

Adhere to a Time Proportion Maintain a Time Allocation Stick to a Time Schedule Observe a Time Ratio

Utilizing a time ratio is an alternative, yet highly effective, approach to time management for individuals who may struggle with sustaining concentration for extended durations. If you are inclined to work in brief intervals of one hour and subsequently find yourself becoming distracted, it may be advisable to capitalize on this circumstance.

The time ratio essentially denotes the allocation of working hours per designated break period. As an illustration, you are operating on a ratio of 1 to 10. This implies that you will engage in continuous work for a duration of 1 hour, followed by a 10-minute period of rest, before resuming work once more. This methodology is widely recognized as the Pomodoro Technique and was formulated by Francesco Cirillo in the 1980s.

The objective of this initiative is to establish a predefined timeframe for your procrastination tendencies, thereby enabling you to effectively manage your time. Attempting to forcibly prolong the duration of uninterrupted work sessions often proves futile. Nevertheless, it is possible to minimize the duration of idle periods. In many cases, individuals who engage in short periods of productivity tend to allocate a greater amount of time to subsequent procrastination. By establishing and adhering to such a boundary, you can acknowledge and admit that you have excessively delayed or postponed tasks.

Using Music

Music is an exemplary method to sustain concentration during cognitive tasks. If one is engaged in composing an essay, completing administrative tasks, or perusing an overdue document, it is advisable to immerse oneself in instrumental music. The compositions of

Chopin or Beethoven would likely produce remarkable results. Binaural beats have also been demonstrated to enhance cognitive acuity and improve memory functioning. In the event that you are engaged in manual activities, such as household cleaning, contemporary music would be the most suitable choice. Select songs that facilitate sing-alongs, as this has a tendency to alleviate the difficulty associated with disliked tasks.

Recognizing the Current Level of Productivity" "Perceiving Your Existing Productivity" "Gaining Awareness of Your Present Productivity

Please consider the following factors, as they will have a significant impact on the level of productivity within your business:

What's Happening Now

Commencing one's day without a structured course of action.

If one commences their day without a well-defined course of action, they are inherently disadvantaged from the outset. Such individuals may find themselves commencing their activities belatedly and experiencing a sense of overwhelming pressure from the onset. Subsequently, you proceed through your day in a state characterized by defensiveness and a sense of urgency in response to emergencies.

You may also find yourself hastily and indiscriminately addressing the concerns and occurrences of others, prioritizing them over your own matters.

No equilibrium

There are seven essential domains in our lives that require the practice of equilibrium in order to cultivate a sense of fulfillment and attain success.

Well-being - the state of physical sensations and the responsiveness of the body to external stimuli

Family and close relations - dedicating time and fulfilling obligations with cherished ones.

Financial - the measure of financial liabilities and income responsibilities

The impact of external stimuli on one's personal and cognitive sphere.

Social - the manner in which individuals engage in interpersonal relationships

Occupational - the methodologies that you employ to enhance your professional trajectory.

Spiritual - denotes one's connection with a higher power and human beings.

Each of these domains necessitates a dedicated portion of our daily schedule, albeit not all can receive an equal amount of time within a single day. It is not imperative to dedicate substantial time to each area, but it is crucial to allocate a limited amount of time to each area.

Ultimately, achieving a well-rounded and harmonious life necessitates dedicating an adequate quantity of time of high quality to each aspect. In any case, should we disregard any of these areas, it is imperative not to underestimate their contribution to our overall success.

As an illustration, neglecting our own well-being can detrimentally impact the welfare of our cherished ones and our social interactions. Similarly, should our financial resources be in a state of imbalance, we will be unable to sufficiently prioritize our professional objectives, aspirations, and other vital areas of concentration.

Cluttered up workspace

An excessively disorganized workspace may give rise to mental clutter.

Issues arise when you are unable to locate vital business documents or access information for your clientele. This substance instigates chaos, generates disorder, and creates confusion, potentially resulting in decreased profitability and postponed invoicing.

Research has been undertaken, demonstrating that an individual in a professional setting, who operates from a desk congested with miscellaneous objects, allocates approximately one to two hours of their daily work time towards examining said items or being diverted by them. This could result in a significant accumulation of wasted hours on a weekly basis.

Poor rest

The main cause of insufficient rest lies in the fact that numerous internet entrepreneurs are unable to achieve their goals or attain results for their businesses. Insufficient sleep can lead to suboptimal decision-making or irrational choices in significant business operations.

Research has indicated that a significant portion, approximately 75%, of internet enterprises experience a lack of sleep, leading to unintentional repercussions on their businesses. Fatigue is detrimental and counterproductive to the domestic responsibilities of an individual.

Should the lack of sleep fail to exert a detrimental effect on the entrepreneur, it will invariably compromise the quality of their sleep. This implies that once individuals attain the opportunity to rest, their sleep is often characterized by fitful and restless periods, primarily driven by underlying stress and other debilitating factors.

Stress-laden days pose a considerable danger to internet entrepreneurs and can eventually prove to be detrimental. The essential component is to amass an adequate amount of rest and appropriate sleep in order to minimize tension and enhance productivity.

Not taking breaks

Engaging in moderate or regular intervals of rest and relaxation could potentially hinder the success of an individual operating as an internet entrepreneur. Due to the absence of a structured or inflexible schedule, individuals in this context perceive that breaks are unnecessary or unattainable. Similarly, they may also hold the perspective that engaging in such activities could potentially be an unproductive utilization of your valuable time. Not truthful. The importance of incorporating regular intervals of rest cannot be understated in achieving daily accomplishments.

Frequently, internet entrepreneurs also fail to take adequate breaks due to their belief that it will enhance their productivity.

They are of the opinion that by working continuously without breaks, they will be able to achieve higher levels of productivity and accomplish more tasks. This does not yield additional outcomes or perhaps a more favorable timeframe.

If the physical state of the individual is depleted, it severely impairs their ability to react and exhibit creativity, thereby negatively impacting the entrepreneur's work standards.

Understanding What Matters

Given your proactive mindset, you can commence arranging matters in accordance with their respective levels of significance.

This is called Prioritizing. Efficient utilization of one's time is of utmost significance, as we often expend excessive amounts of time on nonessential matters and insufficient time on essential endeavors. You devoted an entire hour to engaging in a telephonic conversation with someone regarding their feline companion, thereby foregoing the opportunity to undertake alternative tasks during that period. There is no necessity to prioritize another person's cat over your own welfare or requirements. What shall we do with that extensive pile of dirty dishes residing in your sink? Prioritization entails informing your acquaintance that you are currently unavailable to discuss the topic of the cat, as you must attend to the completion of the household chores.

Although it is understandable that you may have numerous obligations at hand, it is imperative that you establish a certain degree of organization amidst the chaos. What is the foremost task or priority that requires immediate attention or completion? That should be given the highest priority. Subsequently, all other elements can align accordingly.

The primary matter that deserves attention is the initial query that necessitates a response.

Additionally, consider the matters of lesser significance. Is it truly necessary to undertake these tasks? Can it be eliminated without incurring any negative consequences? If that is indeed the case, then commence the removal of extraneous items. If they do not exert any impact on your life or prospects and are deemed removable, then they ought to be.

As an illustration, consider the scenario of owning a collection of aged garments that require transportation to the local thrift store, yet inconveniently situated on the opposite end of the town. It would be illogical for you to undertake the trip today given that you have a scheduled medical appointment nearby and subsequently need to attend an after-school practice to collect your children, which is in the opposite direction. Why engage in excessive haste throughout the day when you could simply arrange an alternative day to deliver the clothes?

Merely possessing a compendium of tasks does not necessitate their completion within a single day.

Distribute the less significant tasks that are capable of being performed at alternative instances. And eliminate any tasks that are unnecessary or can be assigned to someone else.

Subsequently, you simply need to arrange all of your tasks in a sequential manner. Devise a strategic blueprint outlining the method and timeframe for their completion. In the event that your list becomes excessively lengthy or intricate, it is advised to streamline and eliminate items. If you are faced with three to four concurrent or geographically proximate tasks, it would be advisable to consolidate them. In addition to reducing your list, it will also help in saving time. Furthermore, who among us does not require additional time? Once you reach this stage, all the pieces will begin to align.

By giving priority to your tasks, you guarantee that the utmost significance is consistently assigned to their completion. You experience a significant improvement in efficiency while reclaiming your time. This will afford you ample time to pursue your personal preferences, rather than perpetually striving and falling short in completing necessary tasks.

Ensure that when determining your priorities, you consistently allocate some personal time. One does not perpetually have to be constantly in motion. If it is feasible, allocate a minimum of one hour for your personal wellbeing. You hold the utmost importance and are our top priority. Taking proper care of oneself will render other tasks considerably less burdensome.

It is of utmost importance that your happiness remains a priority at all times. It is more effortless to accomplish a task with a pleasant countenance as opposed to attempting it while experiencing fatigue and stress.

Chapter Three: Boundless Drive and Self-Assurance

Indeed, the focus of this chapter will revolve around maintaining motivation and cultivating a sense of confidence.

Motivation is a fundamental element that I am confident everyone is aware of as being imperative for accomplishing tasks. Lack of motivation inevitably leads to procrastination, as it provides no impetus for accomplishing tasks.

However, productivity and accomplishing tasks are rarely commonly associated with confidence.

You could potentially exhibit the same characteristics. You may be pondering the correlation between confidence and productivity.

Dear reader, the matter at hand is closely tied to productivity. Consider the following perspective: In the event that you consistently diminish your own worth, believing that you lack talent or sufficient capability and that greatness is beyond your reach, it becomes apparent that your potential for productivity will be limited. Ultimately, the human body attains what the human mind embraces.

If one repeatedly asserts to oneself that an endeavor is unattainable, one's chances of succeeding diminish significantly. It is as straightforward as that." "It can be ascertained quite easily." "The solution is just that uncomplicated." "It can be summarized in this concise manner.

Nonetheless, should you manage to cultivate a sincere and unwavering conviction, deep within your innermost being, that you possess the capability to achieve the task at hand, you will undoubtedly possess the ability to accomplish it.

Now, I am aware that putting these words into action may prove to be more challenging than expressing them. Confidence is not an attribute that can be spontaneously delivered through an open window and seamlessly assimilated into one's being.

It is not an innate attribute, nor is it hereditary in nature. It is a trait that is obtained through either the impact of one's environment, personal encounters, and social connections, or through diligent exertion.

If you are an individual who has not gained confidence through any of the preceding means, it will be necessary for you to employ the latter approach. You must be proactive in cultivating self-assurance, and that is precisely the area in which I am prepared to offer assistance.

Become confident

Many articles and books discussing the development of confidence often advocate refraining from self-deprecation and cultivating self-belief. Although this advice remains valid, it unfortunately may not prove significantly beneficial to the majority of individuals by itself.

One can attribute this to the fact that the majority of individuals grappling with low self-assurance lack the knowledge or insight required to initiate the process of cultivating self-belief.

When considering the development of self-assurance, two paths may be pursued: the physical pathway and the cognitive pathway. Although both aspects hold equal significance, our detailed discussion will solely revolve around the physical method, as it is the practical step that enables one to initiate their journey towards self-assurance.

Once you have attained proficiency in this matter, you will possess the advantage required to establish a sense of self-assurance through your cognitive processes and to embrace a self-belief, as emphasized in various written publications.

There may be a potential confusion concerning the link between confidence and anything of a 'physical' nature. Although confidence primarily stems from within, one should not discount the potential for external influences to contribute to its enhancement.

Recent research findings indicate that one's posture significantly impacts both confidence levels and overall emotional state.

Undoubtedly, you have undoubtedly observed individuals in your vicinity, carefully attuning to their nonverbal cues, at various junctures.

One can observe individuals who lack proper posture, fail to establish eye contact, and consistently exhibit closed-off body language such as crossed arms or fidgeting with their fingers. These individuals diminish their presence and consistently display signs of fear.

Surprisingly, this specific posture not only imparts an air of inferiority upon these individuals, but also instills within them a genuine sense of inferiority. It induces a sense of diminished self-assurance in them.

Imagine that you have dedicated several hours towards a project that you diligently worked on in the comfort of your own residence. You truly desire to present it to your superior, as you believe it possesses qualities that may garner their appreciation and potentially result in a salary increase or advancement in your position.

As you remain secluded in solitude upon a seat positioned outside his office, patiently awaiting the termination of his discourse with another employee, you are presented with a pair of alternatives concerning your bodily stance.

One could assume a slouched posture, intersect their arms and legs, and cast their gaze downwards, along with displaying various other manifestations of nonverbal cues associated with submissiveness.

Alternatively, you may choose to assume an erect posture, maintaining an expansive chest and a wide-legged stance, while keeping your arms in a relaxed position by your sides.

You may be harboring internal skepticism as you peruse these words, believing that this proposition is implausible in its ability to effect change. However, I assure you that it undeniably does.

There is supporting evidence from various studies that suggests a correlation between adopting 'subordinate' body language and experiencing elevated levels of the stress hormone cortisol, as well as diminished levels of testosterone within the body. Therefore, if such is the manner in which you present yourself non-verbally whilst awaiting outside the office, it is probable that you will persuade yourself that there is little possibility of your boss approving your project. It is highly likely that you will rise and return to your diminutive workstation, carelessly discarding the project in the process.

All the time and effort invested in the project thus far may now be rendered futile, and the future consequences remain uncertain. It is possible that it could have resulted in your promotion.

To provide evidence supporting this claim, a notable investigation was carried out by Amy Cuddy, wherein individuals were invited to a controlled laboratory environment and instructed to assume both the "subordinate" and the aforementioned assertive postures for a brief duration of two minutes. Subsequently, they were inquired about their perceived level of power and provided with the opportunity to engage in a gambling activity. Additionally, an analysis was conducted on a specimen of their oral fluid.

The research revealed that individuals adopting the posture associated with power were observed to have a twenty-six percent higher tendency to engage in gambling activities compared to those embodying the posture associated with inferiority. This disparity in behavior is indeed quite striking.

The adoption of dominant nonverbal cues resulted in a significant elevation of testosterone levels by approximately twenty percent, accompanied by a notable reduction in cortisol levels by approximately twenty-five percent. Conversely, the display of subordinate nonverbal cues led to a decline in testosterone levels by ten percent and an increase in cortisol levels by fifteen percent.

To summarize, it is imperative that you dedicate efforts towards refining your body language in order to cultivate a sense of assurance.

Each day, allocate a few moments of your schedule exclusively for the purpose of honing your ability to assume a confident and commanding posture. Over time, not only will you experience a sense of confidence, but you will also embody confidence.

Once you have effectively refined your confident physical demeanor, mastering your mindset will become a straightforward task.

Now, you have been duly informed of the pivotal element for fostering confidence, the significant stride that will render all subsequent strides noticeably more effortless.

Let us proceed to discourse on motivation at present.

Time Management Brings Selfconfidence

Self-assurance is the instrumental quality enabling us to accomplish significant tasks effortlessly, thereby facilitating the attainment of notable accomplishments with greater ease. Individuals who possess a dearth of self-assurance will encounter challenges when attempting to attain success throughout their lifetime. Self-assurance is akin to a fortified stronghold, rendering even the most formidable individual powerless. Once we have accomplished something using it, we typically proceed to accomplish more with the same level of self-assurance. As a result, our self-assurance is enhanced, leading us to consistently conduct ourselves in a similar fashion or in accordance with our previous behavior. This implies that we adopt a more appropriate demeanor, which in turn instills a sense of self-assurance through effective time management.

The crucial factor in developing self-assurance lies in maintaining an optimistic outlook rather than adopting a pessimistic one. The presence of hope in attaining success engenders the corresponding self-assurance to execute the required tasks. When adopting an optimistic outlook, individuals experience an influx of happiness, increased productivity, and various other positive effects. Typically, this occurs as these attributes bolster one's sense of self-assurance. Conversely, sadness begets a multitude of negative attributes. Individuals with a pessimistic outlook tend to question their aptitude and uncertainly assess their ability to successfully undertake a particular task. They become apprehensive about their tasks. Such doubts create problems. These uncertainties intensify to such an extent that individuals even experience apprehension when attempting to undertake minor tasks. This suggests that the individual's dwindling self-assurance is reflective of their perceived lack of success in the upcoming period. Unfavorable attitudes erect a barrier that impedes the individual's performance and productivity. However, individuals who diligently practice time management exhibit unwavering self-assurance.

Negligence in Time Management Incurs Substantial Consequences.

This attribute is present in individuals who demonstrate a lack of regard for punctuality, lack ambition to attain success, and exhibit no inclination to follow the path to success. These individuals are highly susceptible to experiencing failures and demonstrate a tendency to cause detriment to their surroundings. Individuals of this nature solely engage in receiving without reciprocating. They consistently adhere to prevailing trends, but never establish or pioneer new ones. Gradually, they fade away and no one in this realm survives to perpetuate their memory. Individuals who possess a optimistic outlook on life not only achieve personal success during their lifespan, but also have a tendency to forge significant achievements that serve as guiding beacons for future generations.

Individuals can execute daring feats exclusively within the confines of the circle of death during performances owing to their unwavering self-assurance. Many individuals exhibit the inclination to venture beyond their limits, propelled by their unwavering self-assurance, fully cognizant of their capability to accomplish the task at hand, even if it involves taking considerable risks. They have effectively optimized their time management. They demonstrate a profound understanding of the intrinsic significance of a single second, recognizing that it bears the potential to be the very catalyst for their untimely demise.

Individuals who are employed within the circus industry possess a deep understanding and appreciation for effective time management, as well as an abundance of self-assurance, as they seamlessly command large and powerful creatures such as lions solely with the support of a skilled hunter. Both of these entities possess elements of bravery, enabling them to perform exhilarating feats. However, it must be acknowledged that we are equally capable of achieving similar tasks, as they are also ordinary individuals like us. Should we be able to cultivate a sense of self-assurance and effective time management skills, we, too, will have the ability to accomplish such endeavors.

Individuals who engage in daring feats and exhilarating performances also experience setbacks, primarily attributed to a depletion of self-assurance and a deficiency in the ability to effectively manage time. Hence, it is imperative that we establish self-assurance and effective time management as the foundation of our lives.

Upon examining the determining factors behind an individual's successful life, one can ascertain that self-assurance and effective time management have played a pivotal role. Individuals of such exceptional accomplishments have consistently displayed unwavering confidence in their endeavors, thereby attaining triumphant outcomes.

Individuals who exercise effective time management skills consistently achieve success and possess the ability to accomplish any task. These individuals demonstrate a consistent lack of consideration for pertinent matters when engaging in tasks, displaying a disregard for potential social repercussions. Their singular focus revolves around the attainment of success at all costs. As a result of this inclination, numerous individuals who express criticism eventually develop friendships with them.

In a bygone era, there existed an individual by the name of Steven, renowned for his exceptional wisdom. An individual approached him and inquired how he would respond if confronted by someone who intended to harm him.

In response to his inquiry, he articulated that he has no intention of taking action.

This response was unexpected to him, prompting him to reiterate his query as to why he would not take any action.

Steven affirmed that his fortress is exceptionally robust and impervious to any attempts at breach.

This individual displayed a state of incredulity and inquired regarding the construction of his fortress and its timing.

Steven expressed that his self-assurance and adept time management skills are his prominent assets, possessed only by a select few individuals, from whom fear never arises. They continue to enjoy security and protection within the confines of the fortress.

Witnessing the remarkable self-assurance exuded by Steven, the individual was profoundly impressed. Indeed, the individual in question pertained to the military leader of the opposition, who had initially set forth with intentions to engage in hostile activity but ultimately renounced their pursuit and retreated.

This clearly signifies that the combination of self-assurance and effective time management renders every task manageable, even those that might seem nearly unattainable. Human beings piloting aircrafts, spacecrafts, and successfully accomplishing missions such as space exploration, moon landings, and beyond. All the outcomes are derived from effective time management and a strong sense of self-assurance.

The countenances exuding adept control over time and a strong belief in oneself epitomize the triumphs of individuals of this ilk. Their countenances are brimming with elegance and jubilation. In contrast to individuals of the aforementioned group, pessimistic individuals bear countenances marked by uncertainty and apprehension.

All individuals within this community hold in high regard those individuals who prioritize effective time management, as they serve as a true inspiration to all. These countenances are perceived by individuals as an emblem of authority. Their accomplishments remain obscure, without anyone to bring them to light. These individuals solely serve as a source of inspiration for individuals possessing an inherently optimistic disposition.

Individuals who exhibit adept time management skills demonstrate a highly influential and compelling manner of communication. Their words possess the power to instill encouragement, thereby bestowing happiness and courage upon those they touch. Many individuals often argue that he possesses unparalleled self-assurance, rendering him capable of achieving anything.

Failure

There were two brothers named as Gopal and Mohan. Both individuals were enrolled in the same academic cohort and exhibited exceptional aptitude in their studies. Both individuals dedicated themselves to thorough studying and meticulous preparation for the exams, instilling in themselves a sense of assurance that they would achieve commendable grades and attain top positions. Regardless, as a result of certain circumstances, Mohan's time management was disrupted, leading him to inform Gopal that he will be unable to successfully complete the exams.

Gopal inquired as to why he held such a belief.

Mohan responded by stating his belief.

Following the conclusion of the examination period, the results were released, with Gopal attaining the highest rank and Mohan experiencing an unfortunate outcome as he did not achieve a passing grade. Why? Due to his inability to effectively maintain time management. Notwithstanding the recognition that success is unattainable without effective time management, he veered off course.

Individuals who are incapable of adhering to their time management schedules often begin to question their own capabilities. These individuals are characterized by uncertainty and a tendency to lead others astray from their intended course. When individuals assert that they are incapable of accomplishing this task, they not only diminish their own ability to perform work, but also impede others from doing so. Individuals of this nature experience a decline in their self-assurance and exhibit potentially detrimental behaviors towards society as a whole.

To attain mastery, individuals must possess expert-level proficiency so as to establish a distinct reputation within society. Engaging in sporadic, inconsistent work practices yields only failure and no discernible outcomes.

Effective time management is a commendable attribute that requires individual cultivation. It is not available for purchase through any commercial platform. It can only be cultivated by possessing self-assurance. Once you have determined to pursue a goal, you possess the capacity to accomplish it, for it is at that point that your self-assurance becomes vocal rather than yourself.

Through effective time management, individuals should address and resolve every challenge encountered along their journey. This will enable them to recognize that the task they perceived as challenging actually presented minimal difficulty.

Existence resembles a cyclical phenomenon defined by a sequence of ten interconnected components. Each of us possesses multiple capacities of this nature, although they remain dormant and unutilized.

Effective time management is akin to a potent tool wielded by individuals driven towards achieving success in their lives, capable of resolving their most significant challenges. But exclusively those individuals who possess the intention of attaining success will have the capability to wield this weapon.

www.ingramcontent.com/pod-product-compliance
Lightning Source LLC
Chambersburg PA
CBHW050416120526
44590CB00015B/1982